Nonmonogamy and Death

MORE THAN TWO ESSENTIALS

Nonmonogamy and
Death

Kayden Abley

THORNAPPLE
PRESS

Nonmonogamy and Death
A More Than Two Essentials Guide

Thornapple Press
300 – 722 Cormorant Street
Victoria, BC v8w 1P8 Canada
press@thornapplepress.ca

Thornapple Press is a brand of Talk Science to Me
Communications Inc. and the successor to Thorntree Press.
Our business offices are located in the traditional, ancestral
and unceded territories of the ləkʷəŋən and W̱SÁNEĆ peoples.

Cover and interior design by Jeff Werner
Cover image generated with assistance from wombo
Substantive editing by Andrea Zanin
Copy-editing by Heather van der Hoop
Proofreading by Alison Whyte

Library and Archives Canada Cataloguing in Publication
Title: Nonmonogamy and death : a more than two essentials
    guide / Kayden Abley.
Names: Abley, Kayden, author.
Description: Series statement: More than two essentials
Identifiers: Canadiana (print) 20230549519 | Canadiana (ebook)
    20230549527 | ISBN 9781990869488 (softcover) |
    ISBN 9781990869495 (EPUB)
Subjects: LCSH: Non-monogamous relationships. | LCSH: Death.
Classification: LCC HQ980 .A25 2024 | DDC 306.84/23—dc23

10 9 8 7 6 5 4 3 2 1

Printed in Canada.

To my former partners and metamours—you have helped me grow, trust, love and have faith in life. Thank you for opening my eyes to what could be.

To my beloved spouse—you took a chance on me, even back when I was not sure about nonmonogamy. Now we're married, and I am so happy that you're in my life. You encourage us to be silly and serious and have faith in the world, and to learn from our mistakes.

To the dead—may you be remembered.

Finally, to Rod (1981–2023), who passed away during the writing of this book—you were the kindest, gentlest Unitarian minister and friend a person could ask for. You were much loved and will be missed.

When someone you love dies, and you're not expecting it, you don't lose her all at once; you lose her in pieces over a long time—the way the mail stops coming, and her scent fades from the pillows and even from the clothes in her closet and drawers.

John Irving, *A Prayer for Owen Meany*

The most beautiful people we have known are those who have known defeat, known suffering, known struggle, known loss, and have found their way out of the depths. These persons have an appreciation, a sensitivity, and an understanding of life that fills them with compassion, gentleness, and a deep loving concern.

Dr. Elisabeth Kübler-Ross

Excuse me, do you realize you're going to die? Maybe not today or tomorrow, but *one day*.

Eva Woods, *Something Like Happy*

Contents

Acknowledgements

Thank you to Max, my spouse,
without whom this work would
not have been completed.

Thanks and praise are also due
to Andrea Zanin and Heather van
der Hoop, who tirelessly worked on
editing this short book and helped
shape it from a messy first draft
into a final polished manuscript.

Introduction

One thing that relationships and death have in common is that both of them can creep up on you gradually or crash into you like a lightning bolt hitting a tree during a thunderstorm.

LIFELONG BEST FRIENDS CAN SLOWLY begin to realize they have started developing feelings for each other and have no idea when the new attraction started. Similarly, a person diagnosed with a terminal illness could slowly fade away, with time to prepare for their eventual death. Alternatively, just as love can arrive in a flash of overwhelming emotion, a person could suffer a sudden fatal heart attack, stroke or car accident, leaving their loved ones shocked in the wake of their death.

This book examines a number of connections between relationships and death, specifically regarding nonmonogamy. While monogamous people have many books and resources about death that were created with their specific relationship dynamic in mind, the same cannot be said for those partaking in consensual nonmonogamy. Yet we all must deal with both the emotional and practical aspects of death when we lose a loved one. And people living nonmonogamous lives have additional considerations for which information and support may be scarce.

People practicing consensual non-monogamy have relationships that are, in their very nature, different from their monogamous counterparts—although both monogamous and nonmonogamous relationships should be based on trust, communication, openness, transparency, sex positivity, freedom, care and honesty. For the purposes of this short book, I use "consensual nonmonogamy" as an umbrella term for a relationship structure where people can have multiple romantic, sexual or platonic partners, and everyone involved is aware of and consents to these dynamics. There are as many ways to practice consensual nonmonogamy as there are stars in the sky, and each of them is as valid as the next. (Note that the key here is to practice nonmonogamy in a consensual way—which does not include cheating, coercion, abuse or pressure.) Some people practice solo polyamory or relationship anarchy, while others enjoy hierarchical or non-hierarchical polyamory. People can have multiple partners with different levels of romantic or sexual attachment. Some might identify as monogamish or swingers. Others might identify as nonmonogamous but be single or have only one partner. Some people might identify as nonmonogamous but be closing or opening a relationship for the first time. Some may have been in triads for decades. Some nonmonogamous people may have monogamous partners. In some countries, nonmonogamous people can be married to more than one person at a time.

In this book, my focus is on death in the context of consensual nonmonogamy in the Western world, mainly in Canada. I am a queer, trans, neurodivergent and nonmonogamous person who lives in North America, and who also lived in the United Kingdom for a couple of years while studying Victorian child death and parental grief for my master's degree. I cannot speak to the lived experiences of people in other parts of the world. When I do comment on nonmonogamy and death practices pertaining to any other culture, it is from a purely academic standpoint.

I came to figure out my nonmonogamous leanings through a gradual process, spending time with nonmonogamous friends before becoming involved with nonmonogamous partners myself, and the gradual pace allowed me to learn what did, and did not, appeal to me in nonmonogamy. I dated nonmonogamous people who were married and others who were not; I eventually married my nonmonogamous spouse in autumn 2020, although we had dated and lived together since long before then. Both my spouse and I have had caring partners outside of our marriage. Some are still current partners; others have transitioned to become platonic friends. We are incredibly grateful for having had these people in our lives. We have practiced consensual nonmonogamy with people of varying ages and have learned a lot from every person who has touched our lives.

My journey through the deathcare industry was also multi-faceted and unique. I was fascinated by death and grief at a young age. Growing up, I watched films such as *The Secret Garden*, *A Little Princess* and *Fly Away Home*, all of which deal with family death, grief and loss. I always wanted to help people discuss grief and death, as so many individuals struggle to cope with these experiences. In 2011, I completed my master's degree at the University of Edinburgh in Scotland. I wrote my thesis on child death in Victorian Scotland, examining parental grief across the class systems. Upon returning home to Canada, I enrolled in the Funeral Services Program at Humber College in Toronto, Ontario, where I completed all the coursework to learn how to be a funeral director and embalmer. We studied anatomy, pathology, microbiology and restorative art, along with the art of embalming, to help preserve the bodies of those who had died so they could be prepared for funeral ceremonies, burials and/or cremation. I went into the program not understanding that people don't die in the casket-ready position, lying down on their backs with their eyes and mouth closed and arms crossed over their chests. Funeral homes sent their most complex embalming cases over to the school so we could practice; I worked on individuals who had had complications such as sepsis, bedsores, enlarged limbs due to edema, cancer, malnutrition, dehydration and more. It was certainly a learning experience, and a steep one at that. It soon became clear to me that in some ways, preparing a human body for a funeral was not unlike taking care of the living: we bathed people and washed their hair, massaged the tension out of their muscles, dressed them in their own clothes and treated them with as much respect as we would the living.

The Western deathcare industry can be both unnerving and fantastic for helping deal with the grisly aspects of a death, including embalming a body with the intention of preserving it and making it look acceptable for a traditional funeral. Embalmers can use formaldehyde and other products to preserve a person's body so that out-of-town relatives and friends can attend a funeral days or weeks after the person has died. Skilled deathcare professionals can even make a dehydrated person look more like they did years before their death, allowing the mourners to feel some relief, seeing their loved one's body look clean, peaceful and still, with their eyes closed as if they were asleep. In this way, funeral directors and funeral planning specialists can offer some solace and comfort to the survivors.

That said, based on my experience studying funeral services and volunteering in funeral homes, I can also attest that the modern Western deathcare world is unprepared to help nonmonogamous people with the complex situations they will face when one of their partners dies—or that their partners will face when they die. The modern deathcare industry props up the myth that everyone exists as part of a traditional nuclear family, generally accommodating monogamous couples only, which doesn't help people in other types of relationships. It also did not historically accommodate the LGBTQ+ community, including transgender and nonbinary people. Now, some funeral industry professionals are themselves part of nonmainstream communities, including some who identify as nonmonogamous, and many deathcare professionals will do whatever they can to help people in need, regardless of their sexual orientation, gender identity, relationship status or beliefs. But overall, the deathcare system isn't set up to be inclusive and affirming of people in nontraditional relationships, at least in North America. The situation is also made more complicated by the fact that common-law status is defined and governed by each province and territory in Canada, so each part of the country has a different legal definition of a relationship in which partners are not legally married to each other—and what that means for who gets to make decisions after a partner's death. Similarly complicated laws exist in the United States, where common-law relationships are defined by each state, and in other countries around the world.

People who practice nonmonogamy may or may not have any number of partners; they may or may not be legally married or have children. They and their partners might not live in the same city, country or continent. They may or may not have a supportive network or community nearby to help in the event of an emergency. No two people are the same, and no two relationships are the same. This diversity is beautiful, but its complexity can pose significant challenges for nonmonogamous partners and communities when someone dies.

In an effort to help these marginalized communities navigate the process, this book addresses two main topics. The first is what to consider when you're planning for death in a nonmonogamous setting, including:

- how it differs from monogamous planning for death

- how to approach wills and other legal matters, including what happens if you die without a will

- why it's crucial to determine
  and document who gets custody
  of children if a parent dies

- how to deal with belongings,
  property and debt

- what to consider when making
  burial or cremation plans

The second topic is grief and coping
with death in a nonmonogamous context. I address questions about different
types of partnerships, including nesting
partners, satellite or comet partners,
and types of relationships that do not
exist in the monogamous world. For
instance, how do we grieve the death
of a metamour? What happens when
a polycule collapses due to the death
of one partner? A glossary of terms

relevant to both death and nonmonogamy is provided at the end of the book.

This book can also offer guidance
and support to people who are not
necessarily nonmonogamous themselves, but whose various marginalized
identities may come into conflict
with common death-related Western
traditions—for example, those who are
queer, trans or nonbinary; are not part
of a nuclear family; or are uninterested
in or cannot afford the traditional legal
frameworks surrounding death. In
2023, funerals and the funeral industry
are becoming increasingly expensive,
while wages are stagnant and the cost
of living grows ever higher. People are
having to make unthinkable choices,
not just about their relationships,
but also about their deaths.

I am not a lawyer, and this book
does not constitute legal advice. In

addition, the laws about common-law partnerships and estate planning vary by province and territory, so it's best to consult experts or resources specific to your location for further information. But I hope this book can provide some insight for nonmonogamous people into the complicated world of deathcare and help them avoid some of the pitfalls that could arise. I also hope it helps monogamous people to learn more about the types of situations they may have to navigate in the future among their nonmonogamous loved ones. Finally, I hope it will help funeral directors and other people working in the deathcare field to better support and affirm their clients. More people are coming out as nonmonogamous than ever before, and when they die, their loved ones deserve to feel supported and know that their relationships were—and continue to be—important and valued.

Part 1
Planning for Death in the Context of Nonmonogamy

What's Different for Nonmonogamous People When It Comes to Planning for Death

Nonmonogamous people face many challenges when it comes to the deathcare industry, including legal matters. To my knowledge, as of late 2023, no legislation or case law exists in Canada specific to death in the context of nonmonogamous relationships.

FOR EXAMPLE, THE RIGHTS OF
common-law partners vary widely
across Canada. While the legal
definition depends on the jurisdiction,
a common-law partnership is typically
one in which two people have combined
their households and lived together
continuously for at least a year
without any long separations. In some
provinces, such as British Columbia,
a common-law partner is viewed as
a spouse and inherits at least part of
the estate, even if the deceased didn't
leave a will. However, in Ontario, a
common-law partner is not a beneficiary
of a deceased person's estate unless
they are explicitly named in a will.

Many of the problems faced by
nonmonogamous partners who are not
married to each other arise because
many Western legal systems prioritize
marriage over any other kind of

relationship structure, creating a legal hierarchy. If two nonmonogamous partners are married to each other, they benefit from, and are automatically entitled to, all the legal protections of marriage. Being nonmonogamous does not change the level of protection that marriage affords them. But people in unmarried nonmonogamous partnerships are essentially forced into a hierarchical system that discriminates against them. People might decide to marry in order to protect a partner legally or medically, but having to "choose" one partner to marry goes against the exact ideologies by which many nonmonogamous people live. They might have explicitly tried to avoid such a hierarchical structure, and their other unmarried partners may feel threatened and dismissed by their decision about which partner "deserves" more legal and medical protection. Even when everyone understands and has consented to the decision-making process behind these difficult choices, feelings can be hurt and relationships can be put at risk. Married nonmonogamous people who have other partners they aren't married to must discuss the complexities of these situations with all of their partners. These open conversations allow people to set their expectations and seek out legal or medical support if needed, in order to neutralize or mitigate the hierarchical structure forced upon them.

Partners who don't live together have little legal standing. A common-law partner can typically provide mortgage or rental documentation, joint bank

 accounts or government-issued documents to show they and the deceased partner lived at the same

address. In provinces that recognize common-law relationships, these documents are crucial to establishing rights as a beneficiary if there's no will. However, in the eyes of the North American legal system, nonmonogamous partners who did not live with the deceased would be seen as "merely" friends or lovers, with no legal grounds to benefit from the estate. This realization can be emotionally devastating for nonmonogamous people, especially if they were unaware of these technicalities until after a partner's death.

If you're thinking about and planning for your own or a partner's death, a good early step is to look into the legal framework for death benefits where you live. Understanding the system you're working within is key to estate planning. Nonmonogamous people know their relationships are

just as complete and valid as those of
monogamous people, but convincing
a legal system of their validity can
feel like an insurmountable obstacle.
Having strangers ask you invasive
questions about your personal life can
also feel like an inexcusable trauma.
Some people avoid these conversations
entirely by creating wills and listing
their partners as friends, to prevent
them from having to engage in such
conversations. Another potential option
is to list each beneficiary's name and
social insurance number, address, phone
number or email address to help any
financial or insurance companies track
them down to figure out the legal details
without naming their relationship
to the deceased. Again, it's worth
looking into whether this satisfies legal
requirements where you live. While it's
heartbreaking that many people feel

the need to hide their nonmonogamous relationships, it also makes sense, given that we live in a society where people can be discriminated against for being nonmonogamous. Seeing our relationships be ignored or denied based on our sexuality, gender identity, race, ethnicity, religion and other forms of marginalization can cause discomfort and pain, and can lead to complex trauma and aggravated mental health issues. These negative outcomes could affect people who feel forced to conceal their relationships when adding their partners as beneficiaries, as well as people who find themselves named as friends in a will when they ought to have been named as partners.

Funeral directors and others working in the deathcare industry, such as embalmers, funeral planners, administrative staff, clergy, and so on, can be conservative. They often believe that the purpose of a funeral is to provide support for the surviving family of origin, and place the needs of those family members above those of lovers, friends and other loved ones. Many funeral industry professionals also still believe that a person's next of kin should have the right to deal with them in death. However, a higher-than-average proportion of marginalized people—nonmonogamous and otherwise—are estranged from their families of origin. As a result, this standardized approach can be terribly unfair to people who suddenly have estranged next of kin interfering in their lives, or their beloved partners' lives, without their consent. Even many nonmonogamous people who retain ties with their families of origin may prefer their chosen family to both support them in life and retain decision-making power for them in death.

Medical and end-of-life professionals, including nurses and doctors, might also hold discriminatory views. As they have the power to decide who gets to see the dying person in the hospital or palliative care centre, they can prevent nonmonogamous partners (or any kind of chosen family) from seeing their loved one before they die—even if the family of origin approves of nonmonogamy. Not being able to see a loved one and say goodbye to them in their final moments can have devastating and long-lasting consequences, such as trauma and potentially complex post-traumatic stress disorder.

As humans by nature tend to focus on life and not death, many people concentrate on the joy and companionship they feel within their relationships. They may not discuss end-of-life care options or estate planning. But this avoidance can have major consequences if a partner suddenly dies or experiences a health emergency. One of the easiest and simplest ways for nonmonogamous people to ensure their relationships are recognized in these situations is to make an advance care plan and a will that detail their wishes. They can then update these important documents as necessary if partners and beneficiaries change over time.

Advance Care Planning

Many nonmonogamous people are optimistic about their relationships and their futures, which may lead them to plan for some aspects of their lives and overlook others.

ONE FORMER PARTNER OF MINE offered to add me to her insurance beneficiary list so that if she died, I would be able to avoid worrying about money for a time while I was grieving her loss, which was kind of her. However, she didn't plan for what would happen if she were to end up in the hospital, which was concerning (for her sake, as her next of kin lived in another country). This oversight meant that if anything happened to her, her local chosen family wouldn't have had the legal right to assist her in the hospital or in legal situations, and her family of origin was too far away to make sudden and challenging decisions without difficulty.

This fear is not unfounded. Many people have experienced horror stories when they have been denied access to their dying or deceased longtime partners in hospitals and funeral homes. People who lived through the 1980s may remember many instances of gay men supporting each other through AIDS and its complications, only to be barred from visiting their loved ones during their final days by homophobic families of origin. More recently, my parents, spouse and I have known multiple people in Quebec, Canada, who have been denied access to their partners' hospital bedsides due to the next of kin's homophobia, and in some cases, transphobia and disregard for nonmonogamy. In bigger cities or more progressive parts of the country, the enforcement of anti-discrimination laws and championing of LGBTQ+ rights have helped reduce the potential for these situations. But they may persist in smaller rural areas, where religion may be more prevalent and fewer people may advocate for the rights of the marginalized.

No one should have to die alone or feeling lonely, without their loved ones by their side. The easiest way to prevent this situation is to make an advance care plan, sometimes known as a living will.

While terms and requirements vary based on the laws where you live, an advance care plan typically includes your wishes for health care treatments, such as life-supporting interventions or resuscitation. It also appoints a person who can make health decisions on your behalf if you're incapable, such as if you're unconscious.  Depending on where you live, this person may be known as a health representative, medical proxy or medical power of attorney. An advance care plan allows you some control over how your nonmonogamous partners or friends can support you in the hospital because it identifies who can make crucial health decisions on your behalf. An advance care plan that names one or more partners as health representatives would clearly demonstrate that you want them to be able to visit you in the hospital, even if this goes against the wishes of your family of origin. Once you've created your advance care plan, it's important to make sure your loved ones are aware of it and know where to find a copy so they can follow your documented wishes in case it becomes necessary.

Another aspect of advance planning is appointing a power of attorney, someone who can look after your legal and financial affairs if you become incapacitated. This person could also be your health representative, or you could choose different people for these two roles, which could help signify the importance of both relationships and potentially play to each partner's strengths.

Discussing advance care plans can be difficult, but it's worth pushing through the discomfort to ensure your wishes are well-documented and can be followed. Talking through end-of-life arrangements before the need is imminent allows you to make informed decisions about what you want. It means your partners and other loved ones won't have to wonder about your wishes as they make challenging choices about food or healthcare, medications and their side effects, do-not-resuscitate orders, medical interventions and other challenging scenarios. If you or a partner are receiving end-of-life care through a hospice or palliative care centre, they may be able to refer you to a professional who can support you in these discussions.

Dying without a Will

Many people imagine they have all the time in the world, especially when it comes to a task as potentially time-consuming and expensive as drafting a will.

IT TAKES TIME, EFFORT AND DEEP thought to figure out who should get your property, belongings and money, and who should care for any children and pets. Writing a will also involves deciding how you want your body to be treated, displayed and disposed of after your death. Recent statistics show that 50% of Canadian adults have not written a will or done any estate planning,[1] nor have 59% of American adults.[2] The same percentage of adults in the United Kingdom, roughly 31 million people, had not written a will, according to research from 2020.[3] The lack of a will is particularly harrowing for nonmonogamous people, who might have multiple relationships to consider and many loved ones to provide for and protect. If you have children, it is also paramount to determine who will become their guardian.

If a person wrote a will and appointed an executor before dying, the executor's responsibilities would include making the funeral arrangements and paying for them using funds from the deceased's estate, protecting the property and other assets until they can be distributed among the beneficiaries or sold, and providing the beneficiaries with documentation regarding the estate.

When a person dies without a legal will in place, we say they have died intestate. If a person dies intestate, their estate will be determined by the government to belong to their next of kin. In North America, the government determines what exactly "next of kin" means and how the estate (including property and any money in their bank account) will be allocated. But each jurisdictional government (state, province, county) within each country has different laws defining beneficiaries and allocating estates, so this process can become extremely complicated—another reason it's wise to do some planning for your own death.

When someone dies without having made a will, it puts immense strain on their surviving loved ones, especially if they live in a province or territory that doesn't recognize common-law partners as beneficiaries. Depending on the laws of your jurisdiction, a surviving unmarried partner may need to apply to the court to be granted the right to be the administrator of the estate. The difference between an administrator and an executor is that the administrator can only begin fulfilling duties once the courts say that they can do so—often a time-consuming and expensive process. In contrast, an executor named in a will can begin working on the deceased person's behalf immediately after their death, provided that they get the will and their executor status probated (verified and approved by legal representation).

Dying intestate also means that any additional partners, and any partners who did not live with the deceased, may be left with nothing. This result can come as a frightening shock to non-cohabitating partners, and is an example of how married couples—and cohabitating couples in some provinces—are entitled to certain benefits that unmarried or non-cohabitating partners miss out on. Things can also become complicated if three or more partners live together. To avoid these difficult situations, it is important to consider wills and estates before a crisis occurs.

If crime television shows and movies have taught us anything, it's that death can arrive suddenly, when we least expect it. The best way to protect our loved ones after our death is to make a legal will. If we do not, we will have no control over

what happens with our belongings,
property, money, children and pets.

Making a Will and Planning Your Estate

Nonmonogamous people should know that their ability to determine who has the right to care for their body and make decisions after their death depends entirely on whether or not they have a legal will.

A WILL IS ESSENTIALLY A DOCUMENT that states what you want to have happen to your body, assets (belongings, property, money), and any children and pets, when you die. Laws about wills vary in different provinces and territories, so it's important to look into the rules where you live. Typically, you need to write a legal will yourself (or with the help of a lawyer or notary) and be of sound mind and legal age. You also need to sign the document in ink, in the presence of at least two witnesses, who also need to sign the document as well. Ideally, every adult should have a legal will so that they are not determined to have died intestate.

A will and testament generally contains the following information:

1. Recital: A declaration that you are of sound mind and understand the legal implications of what you are doing.

2. Executor: The name of the person who will oversee the process of

carrying out your wishes as defined in
the will. You should ask this person
if they are willing to serve as your
executor before you name them. You
can also list multiple executors.

3. Debts and expenses: A plan for the
   estate to pay for any outstanding debts
   or funeral expenses, if applicable.

4. Bequests: A list of people or
   organizations to whom you would
   like to leave specific belongings,
   property, sums of money, etc.

5. Guardianships: If you have any minor
   children, other dependents or pets, your
   will should name one or more people
   who will take care of them after your
   death. You should ask these people if
   they are willing to serve as guardians
   before naming them in your will.

6. Remaining property and residual estate: Instructions about what to do with remaining funds and household items (if applicable).

7. Your signature with the date, your address, and any other information required by your jurisdiction (for example, your social insurance number).

8. Witness signatures, addresses and any other relevant information required by your jurisdiction.

Many people believe that creating a will is expensive. And it can be, if you seek assistance from a lawyer. However, an increasing number of affordable alternatives have been introduced in recent years, from do-it-yourself kits sold at office-supply stores to online will preparation services, many of which cost less than $50. These options may be a good fit if you have a relatively simple estate to distribute. However, you may want to seek legal advice if your situation is more complicated, such as if you have children or share property or debt with multiple partners.

Choosing to live your nonmonogamous life privately could mean you don't feel comfortable naming your partners as partners in a will or on other legal documentation. Depending on the laws in your jurisdiction, you may be able to name your partners as beneficiaries without going into the specifics of your relationships with them. That said, not naming them as partners might make it harder for them to receive their assets from insurance companies or financial institutions. One option is to provide additional personal information about the beneficiaries, such as their addresses, phone numbers and even social insurance numbers, to ensure the institutions can confirm that your partners are indeed the people you intended to receive those assets. If you choose not to mention your relationships in your will, it's a good idea to discuss this decision with your partners ahead of time to avoid an unpleasant surprise at an already difficult time.

As long as the legal and medical systems continue to favour monogamous people or lack the provisions to care for nonmonogamous people, nonmonogamous people risk severe consequences when it comes to healthcare and deathcare if they don't plan ahead of time. Many of these consequences can be prevented by creating an advance care plan and writing a will. These documents can help you make sure your wishes are respected and your partners are legally protected in the event of your severe injury, illness or death.

Children and Other Dependents

People who die without having made a will that includes a plan for their children or other dependents may force their loved ones into a nightmarish legal situation.

MANY LEGAL SYSTEMS PRIORITIZE biological ties and lifelong monogamy, which leaves out step-parents, blended families, caring friends, and of course, nonmonogamous parents and their partners. In many jurisdictions, step-parents don't have legal standing in the lives of the children that they're helping to parent, either while the biological parent is alive or after their death. Determining the care and custody of children becomes exponentially more complicated if the biological parent dies without leaving a will and estate plan that details what will happen to their children and who will be allowed to be in their lives.

In many jurisdictions, if a parent dies with minor children in their care, any surviving biological parent automatically gains custody unless otherwise contested. If there is no surviving biological parent and the parent did not name a guardian in a will, the court system will decide on a guardian—and they may not be the person that the parent would have chosen to raise their children.

Being denied guardianship can be especially tragic for the partners of nonmonogamous parents, as they might be completely cut off from the children they cared for, and who cared for them, and would have no say in the children's lives. They might also want to provide financial assistance for the children, but not be allowed to. This scenario can lead to significant stress, grief and trauma for everyone involved.

Another complication is that the children's legal guardian might choose to relocate to another city or country—taking the children with them. Other surviving nonmonogamous partners who feel close to the children, and the children who feel close to the partners, might experience grief and loss due to the separation. This major trauma could leave pain and scars that could affect people all their lives.

Similar situations could arise around the care of adults who are unable to live independently, as well as elders who need support. Guardianship often defaults to any surviving next of kin, and then to a court-appointed guardian, but that person might not be well-suited to provide the appropriate care.

The easiest way to avoid such nightmarish scenarios is to regularly discuss with all the adults involved what would happen in the event of a crisis. Who would look after children or other dependents? In what ways, and how might these responsibilities be divided or shared? Who would the children live with, and when, and where? Who would provide emotional, social and financial support? Ideally, the results of these conversations should be documented in a will, so that those carefully crafted plans can be followed. Parents should look into the legal rules and implications concerning child guardianship where they live so they can ensure their plans fall within them.

Nonmonogamous communities often pride themselves on openness, honesty, good communication and self-awareness, which means they can be havens for communally taking care of children and elders. However, legal custody and responsibilities must be established so that these agreements will stand up to any potential legal challenges and to ensure that everyone involved is on the same page. Discussing potential scenarios and making decisions before a crisis occurs can help avoid adding stress to an already challenging time as everyone navigates a loss.

Assets and Debts (Including Property)

If a nonmonogamous person dies without making a will, they will not have any legal say in who gets to benefit from their estate after their death.

FOR EXAMPLE, THEY WILL NOT BE ABLE to leave money, possessions and other assets to specific partners, friends, charities, or other groups or individuals, or dedicate specific funds to care for any pets or children. If they own a home, they won't be able to say who should inherit it. Dying without a will ensures that strict rules will be followed, no matter the situation of the individual or their family or friends. Instead, provincial or territorial legislation determines how the estate is handled and who will benefit. Having the government sort out who gets a deceased person's assets can be incredibly stressful, time-consuming and even costly for their loved ones, especially if partners live in different parts of the country.

Western laws about death and inheritance are not set up to protect the rights of nonmonogamous partners if someone dies without a will. The only option for nonmonogamous partners of a person who died intestate is typically to hope the next of kin are understanding and allow the surviving partners to become unofficial beneficiaries of the estate. The result can end up being hugely different, even the opposite, from what the deceased person would have wanted.

Another complication is that a person's estate consists not only of their assets, but also of their debts. Typically, these debts must be paid by the deceased's estate before anything can be distributed to beneficiaries. While some debts might be easier to pay off, such as a small amount in credit card debt, others could be much larger and take up a significant amount of the estate—leaving much less than expected for beneficiaries. Sizeable secured debts such as a mortgage or car loan can also lead to stressful situations, especially if ownership of the asset and responsibility for the debt aren't clearly defined.

While financial matters such as assets and debts can be stressful to manage, and even to think about, planning ahead and communicating honestly about money and property is essential. Having these conversations and then documenting the results in a will can help you ensure your assets and finances will be looked after when you die and avoid any surprises for your loved ones.

Writing a will also allows you to specify who should receive cherished personal belongings. Some of these items might not have much financial value, but can be incredibly meaningful keepsakes for surviving partners, friends or other loved ones.

Burial or Cremation Plans

When a person dies without leaving a will, the next of kin gets to determine what kind of funeral to hold, if any, and what happens to the deceased person's body.

THE NEXT OF KIN COULD DENY ANY surviving partners, friends or chosen family access to seeing the deceased after death, or bar them from attending a funeral or memorial service. The surviving friends and partners might not even know that a visitation, memorial service or funeral is taking place.

Also, funerary practices and rituals vary widely in different countries, religions and cultures. For example, I grew up with most of my family based in the United Kingdom, where open-casket funerals are rare; the predominant viewpoint is that the casket should be closed during a funeral so as not to disturb the deceased. In contrast, in many places where Catholicism predominates, such as Italy, it is common for people to have open-casket funerals to say goodbye to the dead; many people also believe that seeing the deceased person's body can provide closure. It's easy to see how the contrast between these two approaches could result in disagreements and hurt feelings. In another example, many people opt for cremation, where the deceased's body is burned and their ashes are later scattered or interred. But choosing cremation can also be challenging for people who were not able to see the body beforehand, as not seeing the deceased person physically to say goodbye may leave them struggling to find closure. Having these decisions made exclusively by the deceased's next of kin may cause great emotional damage if they are in opposition to the wishes of the deceased person or their partners.

Burials and cremation ceremonies can also leave out nonmonogamous partners if the next of kin (or the person who plans the funeral) decides to invite only immediate family or family of origin. This scenario is a real risk if the next of kin doesn't know the person was nonmonogamous or knows but doesn't approve.

Writing a will allows you to document your wishes for your body after death, avoiding potential disagreements between partners and next of kin. Some people go so far as to plan their own funerals, including what music they may want played or where they might want their ashes scattered or interred if they choose to be cremated.

§

Losing a partner is devastating. Dealing with the logistics of sorting out an estate after they die without a will can cause this grief to be more acute, chronic and complicated. To help your loved ones avoid these states of prolonged grief and suffering, it's wise to create a legal will and ask your chosen executor if they're up for the responsibilities of the job.

Every nonmonogamous situation is different. What they have in common, however, is that legal defaults in most parts of the world do not account for their complex realities and are not set up to benefit people in nonmonogamous partnerships in the event of illness and death. While it's wise for everyone to plan for the eventuality of their own death, it's even more of a necessity for nonmonogamous people. These conversations aren't always easy, and the legal measures you might choose to take to lay out your wishes for your estate may end up being costly. But these conversations are a great place to apply all the communication and planning skills that we often need to learn in nonmonogamy. Nonmonogamy encourages us to be honest with ourselves and our partners about our desires, wishes and goals without causing each other to feel isolated or trapped. We are used to speaking truthfully and candidly about relationship dynamics and navigating potentially tough topics, and we can apply our skills to these important conversations. Think of it as one more way of showing love to each other, and ensuring that your loved ones understand what might happen and how to protect themselves and each other.

Part 2
Coping with Death
in Nonmonogamy

While it is often challenging and uncomfortable for people to discuss serious and intense topics, such as death and dying, it is beneficial to have these difficult conversations before they need to happen urgently. As I've emphasized thus far, it's generally far less stressful to try to plan for the eventuality of a death (figuring out wills, end-of-life care, etc.) before it's imminent—or after it happens, when you may need to guess what your loved one would have wanted.

But of course, sometimes a death occurs in a sudden and surprising way, and difficult conversations may need to happen while people are shocked and grieving. Here are some ways to ensure that those conversations go as smoothly as possible.

Conversations To Have after a Death Has Occurred

Have everyone sit down. That way, if anyone gets dizzy or faints from stress, they won't fall from a standing position.

IDEALLY YOU SHOULD BE IN A CIRCLE, such as around a table, and be able to see one another.

Make sure everyone is well-hydrated, fed and well-rested, and that everyone has gone to the washroom. Have beverages and snacks available. Once people's basic needs have been met, they will be able to engage in serious topics of conversation more easily. Many arguments or disagreements (including in my own relationships) have happened because people had not eaten or had not slept well, and did not want to acknowledge it. Often, once we resolved those issues, the discussions went much better, and faster; we became more self-aware and were able to resolve the situations more easily.

Once the conversation around a recent death has been initiated, it is beneficial to give the people involved time to process what is happening and being discussed. Many people, when faced with making decisions after a

 death has occurred, will go into temporary shock and disbelief and may even swear that the deceased person must still be alive. This emotional state can also involve physical changes, including temporary alterations to a person's hearing, vision and ability to breathe or comprehend language. It is best if everyone tries to speak slowly and clearly. Aim to be patient, allowing everyone time to process what is going on and ask clarifying questions or rephrase what was said, to make sure everyone understands.

Some people will react in anger (often part of processing grief), and they need the most support and tenderness. People want to be understood, and they want their loved ones to know that they care about them and are cared for in return. Patience and gentleness in challenging conversations about death, dying, grief and wills can help with that process, allowing everyone to feel seen, heard and cared for.

Once people have absorbed the initial shock of a death, the more challenging tasks can begin. If these decisions are being discussed as a group, it can be useful to designate someone to write down key points of the conversation so that everyone can refer to them later.

Some of the necessary tasks include:

- calling medical professionals. If the death was expected and happened at home, the death certificate can be completed by a nurse practitioner or doctor, who will come to the home to examine the deceased's body. If the death was unexpected, emergency services will have to be

called, and they will determine the
course of action once they examine
the site and the deceased's body.

- contacting other partners, family and
  friends to let them know that the person
  has died. If applicable, ask if they'd
  like to come visit the deceased before
  further arrangements take place.

- consulting funeral professionals about
  any potential services (visitations,
  embalming or cremation, a funeral
  or memorial service, and so on).

- consulting legal professionals to
  look at any wills and estate plans.

Issues for Emotionally Close, Domestic or Nesting Partners

Partners who are emotionally very close may experience forms of grief that are drastically different from partners who are not as emotionally intertwined with each other.

ANY PARTNER IN ANY SITUATION CAN technically experience any form of grief—grief does not discriminate in that way. That said, a partner whose everyday life is highly interconnected with that of the deceased, such as a domestic or nesting partner, may have to handle funeral planning or make arrangements for their loved one's body, which creates a different kind of grieving experience. Alternatively, they may need to deal with their feelings as their partner's next of kin assumes those responsibilities, whether that's because their partner didn't write a will or didn't assign them this role. This scenario can cause stress and hardship if personalities clash or if the partner's next of kin has views on nonmonogamy that are discriminatory or unkind.

The surviving domestic partners will have to resume their everyday lives without their loved one and the daily routines of their partnership—including mundane but meaningful things such as doing the laundry or cooking together. Their everyday lives will be hugely different going forward, and they may struggle to fill the gap left behind.

While nesting partners may carry a heavy burden of grief, they may also have access to the most traditional kinds of support, such as support groups, local friends checking in on them, and so on. However, this support could be complicated if the surviving nesting partners feel they have to keep their nonmonogamy hidden, or feel guilty that they're receiving support while other, non-nesting partners might not be afforded the same courtesy.

Issues for Partners Who Aren't Involved in the Everyday Aspects of the Deceased's Life

Nonmonogamous people in more emotionally or geographically distant relationships will have a vastly different experience when a partner dies.

PARTNERS IN GEOGRAPHICALLY CLOSE, but not emotionally close, relationships may be very affected by their partner's death, but not have as many resources or support structures. Fewer people might have even known about the partner they lost. If the relationship was a very physical one, the surviving partner might suffer greatly when they lose that physical connection. They might experience more physical manifestations of grief, such as touch starvation, a lack of endorphins, headaches or difficulty breathing. Their experience might be the opposite of that of an emotionally attached long-distance partner, who might experience more emotional aspects of grief, such as feeling sad, lonely, angry or isolated, but who didn't have the same physical connection with the deceased partner.

Death also impacts partners in satellite or comet relationships, in which the partners' lives intersect in a joyful, intense, brilliant way while they are together, but then have minimal contact until they see each other again. Such a relationship can occur between partners who live near one another or far apart and could be very important to both partners. But satellite or comet partners might not be invited to assist with funeral logistics, such as deciding what to do with the deceased person's body, planning a funeral or memorial service, and other tasks. This lack of acknowledgement could leave them struggling with feeling the loss of their partner, but not necessarily able to partake in funerary rites or to grieve in the same way as other types of partners. Not every satellite partner would want to partake in such responsibilities, but it's possible that their importance or connection with the deceased could be minimized by other surviving partners.

When someone in a long-distance relationship loses a partner, their daily routines and living spaces will not likely be affected in the same way as someone who lived with their partner. A long-distance partner might want to attend their partner's funeral, but if it's in another city or country, they might not be able to get there—whether due to distance, cost or logistics. Not everyone can afford to take a car, bus, train or plane to another location, even for a funeral. They may not be able to take the time off work; many companies in North America give minimal vacation time in the first place, and will only approve bereavement or compassionate leave for immediate family members. Taking unpaid time off may not be an option, either. In 2023, gas and fuel are getting more expensive, the cost of living is rising on a global scale, and salaries aren't keeping up with those costs. My spouse and I had to resort to going to a food bank for the first time in our lives this past year, and while it has helped us survive on a single income, pay down debt and donate extra food to families in our neighbourhood (feeding six adults and eight children on a regular basis), it means that should I be invited to a funeral in a different city, I most likely wouldn't be able to afford to go.

People tend to shy away from discussing money as much as they shy away from discussing death. Money issues can affect nonmonogamous people in a range of ways, whether or not they're in long-distance relationships, but that's a different book. I bring it up here because missing a loved one's funeral can cause great sorrow and pain, especially if it's due to financial hardship. Some people feel an enormous amount of guilt if they can't afford to grieve in the way they would like to, which complicates the process of grieving. I missed going to my late uncle's funeral due to financial hardship at the time, and I regret the impossible decision I had to make: go, and put myself in more debt, or keep working, to try to keep myself and my spouse afloat financially. My grieving process has also become complicated grief, lasting years instead of weeks or months. Complicated grief can arise when a person pushes aside their grief, either consciously or subconsciously. After not processing it for weeks, months, years or even decades, it finally hits them with major effects on their physical, mental and social well-being. Personally, my grief has lasted years because I was never able to say goodbye in the ways I would have liked to. This experience has made me very sympathetic to similar situations, including in the context of intimate partnerships.

While it might not be feasible for people in long-distance relationships to attend in-person funerary events, saving them a program from the funeral can go a long way to help them feel included and like their relationship is respected. Online memorial events are also a great option. Since the coronavirus pandemic started, online events have become increasingly popular, and they can also allow long-distance partners of a deceased person to be included in funeral planning and memorial ceremonies. Online memorials can also provide a larger nonmonogamy community support base, not to mention helping everyone grieve and heal in due course. Separate funerary events or memorials can also be held for biological and chosen families, if necessary, so that everyone can grieve the person they felt they knew. This option also allows people to keep their private lives private if they wish to do so, allowing everyone to feel comfortable and safe. This privacy is especially important for people in the kink community and other alternative communities, who might not use the same name in those circles as they do with their families of origin or in their professional lives.

Many people, myself included, have also found some solace in writing letters to the deceased person, although those letters will never be sent. Listening to music that reminds them of their loved one is another option. Every time I eat honey, I'm reminded of my uncle, who did beekeeping as a hobby. It gives me comfort and solace and a way to work through some of my grief.

Discrimination within Funeral Services

When I was studying in one of Canada's most academically rigorous funeral service programs, we discussed a few examples of complicated deathcare scenarios, including how deathcare professionals handle deaths involving members of minority communities.

WHILE I TRIED TO DISCUSS nonmonogamy with my professors,

none of them had any experience with the topic, nor had they considered some of the ethical and moral implications for those involved. Sadly, they also didn't seem to care. This negative experience reminded me of discussing the tragic death of a young transgender person with one of my professors, who was also the director of the program. She said that it was perfectly fine to have the trans person's estranged family of origin plan and conduct a funeral where the deceased was named only as their deadname (the name they had been assigned at birth), not by their legally changed chosen name, and wearing clothes of their former gender. As someone who was just starting my transition, I was horrified and saddened. This conversation fuelled my gender dysphoria, discomfort and suicidal ideation, wondering if people would

ever accept me post-transition. The program director's stance—which entrenches disrespect for a trans person's rights and choices, even in death—is utterly offensive to transgender and nonbinary people. Sadly, many funeral industry or deathcare professionals agree with this approach.

Similar problems can arise when it comes to the way the funeral industry deals with nonmonogamy. Deathcare professionals and healthcare professionals need to be more informed about the different ways that people can love and live their lives, including being nonmonogamous, rather than being a final bastion of discrimination in the very moment people most need support and compassion. I hope the healthcare and deathcare industries will eventually accommodate the ways in which societies are changing and evolving. People deserve to be included in funerals and legal documents without hiding who they are or who they love.

In the meantime, my best advice to nonmonogamous people is to be prepared. You may want to ask local marginalized communities for recommendations, or simply speak with funeral directors ahead of time to find one who can offer you a respectful accommodation. If that proves unsuccessful, talk with your partners about how to handle the logistics of hospice or palliative care and funeral arrangements, using the available options and your own creative approaches. We shouldn't have to think about these problems at all—let alone at such a difficult time—but once more, planning ahead can help mitigate the possible negatives.

Grieving Relationships That Do Not Exist for the Mainstream World

Nonmonogamous people can find themselves navigating relationships that monogamous people may not understand or even believe exist.

WHEN A NONMONOGAMOUS PERSON dies, their loved ones may mourn a relationship that goes unacknowledged or is misunderstood by others.

For example, if your metamour (your partner's other partner) dies, it may be challenging to explain to your parent, child, friend or coworker that your partner's partner died. It may be difficult to express how it might affect you or your relationship with your partner. You might have to watch your partner go through all the stages of grief, wanting to help but feeling powerless. You might go through all the stages of grief yourself. You and your partner might go through different experiences of grieving your metamour, which can affect your relationship or your other relationships. The death of a metamour can affect your polycule in myriad ways. If the metamour often assisted your partner (and you) in practical ways, such as buying groceries or making dinner together, the simple task of buying, preparing and eating food can become weighed down with grief. If the connection was more emotional or sexual, your partner might experience dramatic changes in mood, libido or sense of self and other relationships, all of which cause a ripple effect, echoing out and affecting you and others.

Some monogamous people will be able to have empathy and sympathy for your situation, but others will not or may even be indifferent or judgmental. You or your partner might also keep your grief private, which can also be a tough burden to bear and can lead to complicated grief. Monogamous people may understand what it feels like to lose a parent, partner, spouse, grandparent, friend or sibling—but they might not understand what it's like to watch your partner grieve the loss of their other partner, or for you to grieve the loss of your polycule.

This is one reason that being part
of a community of nonmonogamous
people can be really useful and life-
affirming. A supportive network of
people who understand and accept your
relationship structures without need
for explanations and who are uniquely
equipped to understand some of the
challenges you face as a nonmonogamous person can make an enormous
difference at such a difficult time.
Nonmonogamous people know, more
than many others, that relationships
can be long and complex, or short
and fleeting, or anything in between.
They know that they may not have
forever to care for others and be cared
for in return. And they understand
the nuances of these relationships,
and that their length or proximity
does not dictate their importance.

It can also be helpful to work with a trauma-informed, nonmonogamy-friendly therapist. Not all mental health professionals specialize in grief and trauma—it's best to find one who does, who can provide emotional support and direct you to other resources for help.

Grief and Its Many Forms

After a death, it is important to process your emotions and take the time to grieve the lost relationship.

IT'S USUALLY A GOOD IDEA TO MOVE through part of your healing journey before starting any new relationships so that you avoid placing all your emotional needs onto a new partner. People who have not worked on their healing, who are still grieving previous losses, can unintentionally destroy new connections and relationships. Their pain and grief may cause them to act in unstable ways: lashing out, closing themselves off and holding their emotions in, freezing or shutting down when serious conversations are brought up, being unable to help the other person but needing help in return—these are all legitimate parts of grieving, but they can place a lot of pressure on a new connection.

Ideally, nonmonogamous people can aim to avoid such situations by being part of nonmonogamous communities, through which they can surround themselves with multiple caring relationships and connections. They can foster each connection with integrity and generosity, finding support in times of hardship and grief. When one of those connections is severed, they can rely on the others to help them get through the hardship. They learn to understand that life goes on, even when they might wish otherwise, and that losing a relationship can be utterly devastating but does not necessarily mean the end of the world. More partners mean more potential for grief, as there are more people involved, but also more potential for support, should a loss occur. Nonmonogamous communities are aware of how nontraditional relationships can benefit a person, and how they can support you should things go wrong, including if you lose a partner. Support could mean spending time with your polycule or other nonmonogamy-friendly people, including talking, going on walks in silence or doing a new hobby. It could also mean having someone come over to help you clean your house or make meals, should those tasks prove too difficult in the face of grief. Many nonmonogamous people find it helpful to be part of a local or virtual nonmonogamy group, where they can give and get support as needed.

Many people from different alternative communities, including nonmonogamous ones, may find that their experiences aren't reflected in media or the discussions they see around them. In most contexts, we in North American society make space for people to grieve the loss of their parents, but hold little space for estranged or abused adult children who are relieved when a parent dies. We make space for people to grieve immediate family members, but hold little space for people to grieve more distant relatives (say, a niece or cousin), even if those relationships were extremely close. This disconnect is reflected in many companies' benefit packages for compassionate leave or bereavement leave, which often list the immediate family members whose deaths "count" enough for the employee to take time off. People are allowed, and encouraged, to grieve a spouse or long-term nesting partner, but less support exists when grieving someone with whom they had a nontraditional relationship. Grief can be incredibly traumatic, and it can be harder when society at large does not recognize or approve of your relationships or partners, particularly when it comes to getting time off work or finding appropriate support groups to process the loss of your loved one.

Dr. Elisabeth Kübler-Ross became famous for her discussions on what she saw as five distinct stages of grief: denial, anger, bargaining, depression and acceptance. While the idea of the stages as distinct steps in a linear progression became popularized, she actually described them as potentially overlapping, repeating or cyclical experiences. She was also describing the experiences of people who were themselves dying, not those who were grieving a lost loved one—similar experiences, but not identical.

Grief is often complicated and does not necessarily progress in a linear timeline, instead ebbing and flowing and changing over time. Nonmonogamous people might also experience more complex challenges in their grieving process if they can only be open about it with certain people. For example, not everyone has the financial or class privileges to be open about their nonmonogamy to their bosses or coworkers, as they might be at risk of discrimination. Having to force a part of one's life into the closet can create inner turmoil and may even result in physical or mental illness, such as anxiety or depression. Grief counsellors and therapists now know that such scenarios can lead to complicated grief.

People can also mask their grief. Neurodivergent people sometimes mask their neurodivergent traits for the sake of neurotypical people's comfort, which can cause a lot of stress and fatigue. Similarly, people who mask their grief appear to show no outward signs of grief, keeping it all inside, often to their detriment. People who mask grief may appear fine to the casual observer, and will only admit when pressed that they are suffering. In some cases, keeping their grief private might allow the grieving person to work on their healing, but for others, masking their grief is the only way they can manage to keep going and survive.

Grief may come in waves—a tiny wave can be bearable, but a

large wave can knock a person over without warning. Some people find it challenging to eat, sleep or talk when in the process of grieving. To cope, and to heal, you might write letters to the deceased and burn them, bury them in a garden or keep them in a desk drawer. You might perform any activity with the deceased person in mind. You might think of your loved one whenever you hear a certain song, smell a certain scent, or taste a familiar food. Literature, music, dance, food, nature and even people can remind us of those who have left us. And some people even find solace in forgetting.

You can mourn the dead however you choose. While doing so, if you're lucky, you might also deepen other relationships, find new friends and people to connect with, or discover new hobbies or activities, all of which can offer support and help lessen the burden of grief in time. You may find that your sorrow leaves you altered from the person you once were.

That's normal. Community, patience and time can soften the challenges of grief, but it often stays with us for the long term. Coping skills and support can help it become more bearable. Give yourself time and space to heal. Others will understand if you struggle while trying to enjoy life again in a healthy way. Everyone has their own trajectory when it comes to grieving, and their own emotions and experiences to work through—and that is nothing to be ashamed of.

Conclusion

Consensual nonmonogamy can offer many strengths to people who are dealing with death, dying and grief.

NONMONOGAMOUS COMMUNITIES strive for self-knowledge and strong communication skills. Nonmonogamy helps us develop planning skills (such as those needed to schedule dates with multiple partners) and the ability to have clear, open, honest conversations that take into account the needs and desires of multiple people. All these skill sets and practices can help when dealing with death and grief in a proactive way. As well, consensual nonmonogamy allows us to build an uncommonly broad support structure, in terms of our relationships and community, to support one another as we deal with illness, death and grief.

I hope you can use these rich strengths and advantages to help you cope with the practical and emotional challenges of dealing with death in a nonmonogamous context, now or in the future. Relationships help make the unbearable parts of life enjoyable. Please tell your loved ones that you care about them while you still can. Enjoy life, but also plan ahead to make navigating your death as smooth as possible for your loved ones, and encourage them to do the same.

Notes

1   "Lacking the Will: Half of Canadians Say They
    Don't Have a Last Will and Testament, including
    One in Five Aged 55+," Angus Reid Institute,
    accessed August 30, 2023, https://angusreid.org/
    canada-will-testament-intestate-dying-without-will/.

2   PRNewswire, "More Than Half of Americans Don't
    Have a Will, Says New Survey By FindLaw," news
    release, August 15, 2023, https://www.legalwills.ca/
    news_994_010815.

3   "31 Million UK Adults Don't Have a Will in Place,"
    Canada Life, published September 25, 2020,
    accessed May 13, 2023, https://www.canadalife.
    co.uk/news/31-million-uk-adults-don-t-have-a-will-
    in-place.

Glossary

Casket: A rectangular box, typically made
of wood or metal, into which a deceased
person is placed for the purposes
of burial, cremation or a funeral
ceremony. Casket lids have a hinge and
are often cut in two pieces so that the
deceased can be seen from the waist
up in an open-casket funeral. North
American funeral homes generally
use caskets, as opposed to **coffins,**
which are more frequently used in the
United Kingdom and other countries.

Chosen Family: The people that someone has chosen to have in their lives, such as partners, friends and others, who are as meaningful to them as traditional biological family members—and sometimes, more so.

Coffin: A long hexagonal box, typically made of wood, into which a deceased person is placed for the purposes of burial, cremation or a funeral ceremony. Coffin lids can be removed completely for viewings.

Cremation: The process by which a deceased person's body is burned, usually following a funeral ceremony, until they have become ash. Cremation typically occurs at a crematorium, although some cultures, including some in India, do open-air cremations. The ashes are typically given to the deceased's **next**

of kin, unless otherwise specified in a will, and are then kept ceremonially or scattered in a meaningful place.

Embalming: The cleaning, preservation and restoration of the deceased's body for **funeral** purposes. Typically, modern-day embalmers perform such tasks as washing the body and hair, massaging the rigor out of the muscles, closing their eyes and mouth, laying them on their back with their arms positioned across their torso, dressing them and styling their hair. Embalmers also preserve the deceased's body with chemicals, allowing a funeral service to be delayed for weeks (which can help distant loved ones attend). If the funeral is open-casket, embalming allows people to see their deceased loved one, which can help them process the death and grieve.

Estate: A person's assets at the time of their death, including their bank accounts, investments, property and belongings.

Funeral: A ceremony, usually with the deceased's body present in a coffin or casket, to commemorate their life. It is usually attended by **next of kin**, family members, friends, **chosen family**, coworkers and other people who wish to celebrate them. Funerals typically take place a short time after the deceased's death.

Funeral Director: A paid professional in the deathcare industry who makes funeral arrangements for the deceased. Their tasks can include embalming, coordinating the funeral ceremony or cremation, pre-planning a funeral, offering grief counselling for survivors or assisting with the legal matters, although not

every funeral director will perform
every task. Also known as a mortician.

Grief: A profound sadness and distress
caused by bereavement and mourning
a death or loss. Grief can gradually
become less intense and raw and allow
the grieving person to eventually
cope with the loss, but it can also
ebb and flow in complex ways.

Intestate: A person is said to have died
intestate when they die without
leaving a **will** that explains how they
wish to have their **estate** distributed.
If someone dies intestate, their
assets will be distributed based on
the laws of their jurisdiction.

Memorial: A ceremony to commemorate
the deceased's life, usually without the
body present, or present post-cremation

as ashes. It is usually attended by **next of kin**, family members, friends, **chosen family**, coworkers and other people who wish to celebrate the deceased person. Memorials can take place a short time after the death, but can also take place weeks, months or even years later.

Metamour: A person's partner's partner. Metamours may be friends or acquaintances, or may have no other interactions, but by definition they must know of each other's existence and consent to the relationship dynamics in place between each of them and their shared partner.

Nesting Partner: The partner a person lives with on a long-term basis. Some nesting partners are married, while others are not; some have children together, while others do not; some share finances, while others do not. Also known as a domestic partner.

Next of Kin: A person's closest living relative(s), either biological (such as a parent, sibling or other blood relative) or legal (such as a spouse or an adopted child). Generally, if the deceased has not written a legal will, the next of kin will be the legal beneficiary by default. This designation gives them custody of the deceased's body, assets, property and debts, and potentially guardianship of any children or pets, although the exact legalities vary by country and province (or state or county).

Polycule: A relationship structure consisting of a person and their partner(s) and **metamour**(s).

Probate: The process of the legal courts accepting and validating a will, or in the absence of a will, approving or appointing an executor to the deceased's estate.

Satellite Partner: A partner who is at an emotional and/or physical distance from the nesting relationship(s) but still supports their partner in various ways.

Will: A written legal document that discloses a person's wishes as to what will happen to their body, assets, debts and property after their death, as well as any children or pets they may have.

Bibliography

Angus Reid Institute. "Lacking the Will: Half of
    Canadians Say They Don't Have a Last Will
    and Testament, including One in Five Aged
    55+." March 7, 2023. Accessed August
    30, 2023. https://angusreid.org/canada-will
    -testament-intestate dying without-will/.

Anonymous. "How Polyamory Helped Me
    Survive Widowhood." *Chatelaine*.
    September 7, 2021. https://www.chatelaine
    .com/living/polyamory-widowhood/.

Canada Revenue Agency. "Canada Revenue
    Agency – What to Do Following a Death."
    Government of Canada. June 22, 2017.
    Accessed May 4, 2023. https://www.canada.ca
    /en/revenue-agency/services/forms-publications
    /publications/rc4111/canada-revenue-agency-
    what-following-a-death.html#P51_5727.

Canada Wills. Accessed July 16, 2023.
   https://www.canadawills.com/.
Cassidy, Mel. "Grief and Non Monogamy."
   Radical Relationship Coaching (blog). August
   18, 2021. https://radicalrelationshipcoaching
   .ca/grief-and-non-monogamy/.
"Colours of Mourning Around the World."
   Funeral Guide (blog). October 26, 2017.
   Accessed June 25, 2023. https://www
   .funeralguide.net/blog/mourning-colours.
Davis, Simon. "Death Is Way More Complicated
   When You're Polyamorous." *Vice.*
   November 9, 2015. Accessed May 13,
   2023. https://www.vice.com/en/article
   /3bj4d5/death-is-way-more-complicated
   -when-youre-polyamorous-511.
Davis, Simon. "Transgender People Are
   Misgendered, Even in Death." *Vice.* January
   21, 2015. Accessed June 1, 2023. https://www
   .vice.com/en/article/exm3v4/transgender-
   people-are-misgendered-even-in-death-120.
Doughty, Caitlin. *Smoke Gets in Your Eyes: And
   Other Lessons from the Crematorium.*
   Edinburgh: Canongate Books, 2014.
"Dying without a Will in Canada." Willful.
   Accessed May 13, 2023. https://www.willful
   .co/learn/dying-without-a-will#:~:text=If%20
   any%20of%20your%20children.

"Everything You Need to Know about
     Inheritance Law in Canada." Willful.
     Accessed May 10, 2023. https://www
     .willful.co/learn/inheritance-law-canada.
Fern, Jessica. *Polysecure: Attachment, Trauma
     and Consensual Nonmonogamy*.
     Portland, OR: Thorntree Press, 2020.
Feste, Shana, dir. *The Greatest*. 2009. Paladin.
Funeral Guide. n.d. https://www
     .funeralguide.co.uk/.
Government of British Columbia. "Advance
     Care Planning." Accessed August 30,
     2023. https://www2.gov.bc.ca/gov
     /content/family-social-supports/seniors
     /health-safety/advance-care-planning.
Government of British Columbia. "After a
     Death: Who to Notify When Someone
     Dies." Accessed May 13, 2023. https://
     www2.gov.bc.ca/gov/content/life-events
     /death/after-death/who-to-notify.
Government of British Columbia. "Wills and
     Estates." Accessed August 30, 2023.
     https://www2.gov.bc.ca/gov/content
     /life-events/death/wills-estates.

Gouvernement du Québec. "Distribution of
the Inheritance in a Legal Succession
(Table)." Last modified February 23,
2023. Accessed May 13, 2023. https://
www.quebec.ca/en/justice-et-etat-civil
/testament-succession/succession/settlement
/death-without-will/distribution-table.

Grollman, Earl A. *Living When a Loved
One Has Died*. 2nd ed. Boston,
MA: Beacon Press, 1987.

Jokinen, Tom. *Curtains: Adventures
of an Undertaker-in-Training*.
Toronto: Vintage Canada, 2011.

Klein, Jessica. "Ethical Non-Monogamy: The
Rise of Multi-Partner Relationships."
Lovelife (blog), *BBC*. March 25, 2021.
https://www.bbc.com/worklife/article
/20210326-ethical-non-monogamy-the
-rise-of-multi-partner-relationships.

Klein, Jessica. "The Invisible Obstacles of
Non-Binary Dating." *Lovelife* (blog),
BBC. June 2, 2022. https://www.bbc
.com/worklife/article/20220601-the
-invisible-obstacles-of-non-binary-dating.

Klein, Jessica. "The Millennials in Sexless
    Marriages." *Lovelife* (blog), *BBC*.
    October 20, 2022. https://www.bbc
    .com/worklife/article/20221019-the
    -millennials-in-sexless-marriages.

Klein, Jessica. "The Rising Curiosity behind
    Open Relationships." *Lovelife* (blog),
    BBC. August 5, 2022. https://www.bbc
    .com/worklife/article/20220725-the-rising-
    curiosity-behind-open-relationships.

"Know Your Rights When Someone Dies
    without a Will." Dial-A-Law, People's
    Law School. Accessed May 13, 2023.
    https://dialalaw.peopleslawschool.ca
    /when-someone-dies-without-a-will/.

Labriola, Kathy. *The Polyamory Breakup Book*.
    Portland, OR: Thorntree Press, 2019.

Mayer, Robert G. *Embalming History,
    Theory, and Practice*, 5th ed. New
    York, McGraw-Hill, 2011.

McIntosh, Matt. "What Happens If You Don't
    Have a Will — By Province." Farm
    Credit Canada. Accessed May 6, 2023.
    https://www.fcc-fac.ca/en/knowledge
    /dont-have-a-will-by-province.html.

Memoria. Accessed April 26, 2023.
    https://www.memoria.ca/.

Mullins, David. *Pathology and Microbiology for Mortuary Science*. Clifton Park, NY: Cengage Learning, 2005.

Petch, Alison. "Funeral and Mourning Clothing." England: The Other Within. Accessed May 13, 2023. https://england.prm.ox.ac.uk/englishness-funeral-clothing.html.

"Polyamory Is Getting Slivers of Legal Recognition in America." *The Economist*. January 12, 2023. Accessed May 13, 2023. https://www.economist.com/united-states/2023/01/12/polyamory-is-getting-slivers-of-legal-recognition-in-america.

PRNewswire. "More Than Half of Americans Don't Have a Will, Says New Survey By FindLaw." News release, August 15, 2023. https://www.legalwills.ca/news_994_010815.

Ravenmaid37. "Advice Needed: Metamour's Death and Aftermath." Forum post on Polyamory. September 18, 2017. Accessed May 13, 2023. https://polyamory.com/threads/advice-needed-metamours-death-and-aftermath.92823.

"Right to Inherit and Receive Support from
Common-Law Spouse's Estate upon
Death." Legal Line. Accessed May 13,
2023. https://www.legalline.ca/legal-answers
/right-to-inherit-and-receive-support-from-
common-law-spouses-estate-upon-death/.

Roach, Mary. *Stiff: The Curious Lives of
Human Cadavers*. New York: W.
W. Norton & Company, 2003.

Romanek, Mark, dir. *Never Let Me Go*.
2010. Fox Searchlight Pictures.

Shelby. "Non-Monogamy Terms Explained."
Respark (blog). June 15, 2022. Accessed
June 10, 2023. https://respark.co/blog
/non-monogamy-terms-explained/.

Stone, Douglas, Bruce Patton, and Sheila
Heen. *Difficult Conversations: How to
Discuss What Matters Most*. 2nd ed.
New York: Penguin Books, 2010.

"31 Million UK Adults Don't Have a Will in
Place." Canada Life. Published September
25, 2020. Accessed May 13, 2023.
https://www.canadalife.co.uk/news/31
-million-uk-adults-don-t-have-a-will-in-place/

"What Happens If You Die without a Will
 in Canada?" IG Wealth Management.
 November 10, 2022. Accessed June 10,
 2023. https://www.ig.ca/en/insights/what
 -happens-if-you-die-without-a-will-canada.
Woods, Eva. *Something Like Happy.*
 Toronto: Graydon House, 2017.
Young, Kevin. *The Art of Losing: Poems
 of Grief and Healing.* New York:
 Bloomsbury Press, 2013.

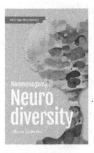

It's Called Polyamory: Coming Out About Your Nonmonogamous Relationships

Tamara Pincus and Rebecca Hiles, with a foreword by Kendra Holliday

"Doing poly, holding poly space in the world, is hard work, often thankless. Thanks to this wonderful resource, it's now a lot easier."
    — Loraine Hutchins, co-editor, *Bi Any Other Name: Bisexual People Speak Out*

Ask Yourself: The Consent Culture Workbook

Kitty Stryker, with a foreword by Wagatwe Wanjuki

"*Ask: Building Consent Culture* editor Kitty Stryker invites readers to delve deeper, with guest experts and personal anecdotes, to manifest a culture of consent in one's own community that starts at the heart."
    — Jiz Lee, editor of *Coming Out Like a Porn Star*

Ask Me About Polyamory: The Best of Kimchi Cuddles

Tikva Wolf, with a foreword by Sophie Labelle

"The warm and open style, and great way of getting complex things across simply, makes it one of the best relationship comics out there."
— Dr. Meg-John Barker, author of *Rewriting the Rules*

Love's Not Color Blind: Race and Representation in Polyamorous and Other Alternative Communities

Kevin A. Patterson, with a foreword by Ruby Bougie Johnson

"Kevin does amazing work both centering the voices of people of color and educating white folks on privilege. His words will positively influence polyamorous communities for years to come."
—Rebecca Hiles, The Frisky Fairy

Kayden Abley (they/them and he/him) is an Ottawa-based queer, nonbinary and transgender healthcare admin worker and freelance author/publisher who has been published in the anthologies *Amanda Goes To Italy* (Girls Gone By Press) and *Under The Poet Tree* (Pedlar Press) and *Mosaic* literary magazine. They hold a diploma in Fine Arts from Dawson College, a BA (Hons) in Celtic Studies from the University of Toronto and a master's degree in Scottish Studies from the University of Edinburgh. They also completed the academic portion of Humber College's Funeral Services Education program, where they studied grief counselling, funeral law and funeral planning among other topics.